# BY PAUL HORGAN

### NOVELS

The Fault of Angels
No Quarter Given
Main Line West
A Lamp on the Plains

Far From Cibola
The Habit of Empire
The Common Heart
Give Me Possession

A Distant Trumpet
Mountain Standard Time (*a collected volume
containing* MAIN LINE WEST, FAR FROM CIBOLA, *and*
THE COMMON HEART)

### OTHER FICTION

The Return of the Weed
Figures in a Landscape
The Devil in the Desert
One Red Rose for
    Christmas

The Saintmaker's Christmas
    Eve
Humble Powers
Toby and the Nighttime
    (*juvenile*)

Things As They Are

### HISTORY AND BELLES-LETTRES

Men of Arms (*juvenile*)
From the Royal City
New Mexico's Own Chronicle (*with Maurice
Garland Fulton*)
Great River: The Rio Grande in North American History
The Centuries of Santa Fe
Rome Eternal
Citizen of New Salem
Conquistadors in North American History
Peter Hurd: A Portrait Sketch from Life
Songs After Lincoln

# SONGS AFTER LINCOLN

## by Paul Horgan

NEW YORK
FARRAR, STRAUS AND GIROUX

811
H

FOR ANDY AND BETSY
*one hundred years after the death of*
*Abraham Lincoln*

# CONTENTS

PROEM : *The Catafalque*      *xiii*

I. THE WAR

1. *Daybreak Over a Battlefield*      *3*
2. *Far Battle*      *5*
3. *Pinned Down*      *6*
4. *Tintype of a Private of the Fifteenth Georgia Infantry*      *7*
5. *Commander Death*      *8*
6. *A Candle in the Ward*      *10*
7. *Last Words in a Soldier's Diary*      *11*
8. *Endless Autumn*      *12*
9. *One Man*      *13*

II. THE CASUALTY

10. *The Farmer's Wife*      *17*
11. *The Farmer*      *19*
12. *The Neighbor*      *21*
13. *Spring Water*      *23*
14. *The Lost Son*      *24*

15. *The Enemy*　　*28*

16. *The Fellow Soldier*　　*29*

17. *Coursing Rivers*　　*35*

18. *The Soldier's Sweetheart*　　*37*

19. *The Soldier's Child*　　*38*


III. THE PRESIDENT

20. *Respect*　　*41*

21. *Father Abraham and the Recruit*　　*42*

22. *Wartime Evening—The White House*　　*45*

23. *The Schoolboy*　　*46*

24. *Duncan and Mr Lincoln*　　*52*

25. *The Dreaming Slave*　　*53*

26. *Reviewing Negro Troops Going South through Washington, April 26, 1864*　　*57*

27. *The Hill*　　*58*

28. *Biography*　　*59*

29. *Thought of Mary Lincoln*　　*61*

30. *A Veteran's Memory*　　*62*

31. *The Last Photograph, April 9, 1865*　　*63*

POSTLUDE: *Glory*　　*65*


NOTES AND COMMENTS　　*69*

# SONGS
# AFTER
# LINCOLN

## PROEM: The Catafalque

*Often in my childhood I would stand*
*In the Buffalo Historical Museum*
*Next to a long and gently tilted framework*
*Draped in black, and I once put my hand*

*Upon its dusty moth-dried shape and breathed*
*The sorrows of a half century before,*
*For it was Abraham Lincoln's catafalque*
*On which for a grieving pause he was wreathed*

*In my city's homage before I was there,*
*On his way home forever to Illinois,*
*And, visiting the fact of the President dead,*
*I saw his lifetime in my timeless stare.*

# 1.

# *The War*

# 1. DAYBREAK OVER A BATTLEFIELD

Bushes bronze
Like a fox's brush,
Sumac afire in
Forest hush,

Day-blue smoke
Against the hills,
Grains of frost
Along the rills,

Fields of rye
Unfaded green,
Skeins of cloud
Lofting serene,

Cool in the air
To make a heart
With morning's waft
Catch and start,

And nothing moves
On the sky
But carrion birds
Over where they lie,

Yesterday's fallen,
Whose given breath
Far children draw
To outlive death.

## 2. FAR BATTLE

The field is gold
With the drift of spent leaves.
Summer's hold
Has failed within the trees.

As, from far away,
If you see children running,
All their play
Is ambush and cunning,

So, seen afar,
Lines of running soldiers
Give to the War
And its opposing gestures,

Aspect as innocent
As childhood's sham battle,
Though it be evident
This engagement is mortal.

## 3. Pinned Down

I was in the dust,
With every breath I drank it,
And burrowed as I must
Into the earth to thank it

For keeping me concealed
Below the roof of lead
That flew across the field
Close above my head.

I got there by a blunder,
I awaited a command,
But only my heart's thunder
Sounded in the land.

Would I lie there forever?
When might I rise and run?
Never, never, never,
When they blew out the sun.

## 4. Tintype of a Private of the Fifteenth Georgia Infantry

Lynx-eyed, cat-quiet, sleepy mild,
He could seem a wary child,
His tilted head a little turned
Like one who very early learned
Of unexpectedness in life.
But the blade within his knife
Is the razor temper in his bone
Which he never had to hone
To edge it ready for the kill.
Surely light-voiced, lounging still,
Southern-sweet at mouth and brow,
Once provoked, he'd show you how
In an instant he could spring
To be the death of anything.
The yellow gaze in his sighting eye
Will never flick when his bullets fly.

## 5. Commander Death

*Around the cot*
*of a dying soldier*
*they have set a standing screen*
*in Death's honor.*
*Behind the screen*
*Commander Death*
*is waiting*
*for his dear one.*
*No one knows*
*when he will give the order*
*to go with him.*
*The mosquito curtains*
*along the rows*
*of hospital beds*
*seem to hover*
*like patches of mist.*
*All down the ward*
*the other wounded*
*and the sick*
*and the hopeful*
*turn their backs*
*upon the screen.*
*They play*
*games of cards,*
*tell riddles,*
*read letters aloud,*
*one softly drums on a banjo.*

*Lest Death*
*be a contagion*
*the patients*
*exaggerate*
*their trivial acts of life.*

Have I come awake?
What is so far away,
So far away along the dark,
The dark airless ward, a ray,
A ray of fire, or a spark,
A spark that sets an ache,
An ache inside my head?

Am I awake or am I dead?

What can be done?

Will no one ever stay
To help me try to pray,
Or lean over to explain
About the light, about the pain,
For they are one . . .

Oh will the day
Never break?

## 7. Last Words in a Soldier's Diary

"Dear Brother Thomas, I have been brave
    But wicked—pray for me."
*While there is breath I would save*
    *My perilled eternity.*

"Dear Brother Thomas, I have been brave
    But wicked"—*no one knows*
*All the sins that held me slave*
    *Which Time could not disclose.*

"Dear Brother Thomas, I have been brave"—
    *And will that help me now?*
*The deeds I mourn will fill my grave*
    *As my length may allow.*

"Dear Brother Thomas"—*innocence*
    *I took to war with me.*
*Now prisoned by experience,*
    *I beg you pray me free.*

"Dear"—

## 8. ENDLESS AUTUMN

Autumnal, all-expecting frost and the still
Fall of brittling leaves to silvered earth,
The dying fall of hunger for sleep, the hill
Itself returning to its valley birth—

Along its bed the creek goes ever lower
And lower still to find the embosoming sea,
And far and fading the forest air is bluer
The farther it hangs in the distance tree by tree—

The summer humming web of meadow bees
Has flown in a golden draught of long drawn air,
The stalks turn crisp to stand until they freeze,
And the long time of dying is on the year—

The harvest moon is the last red moon till snow,
And the blue cloak of heaven is cold to see,
And smoke rising from battle seems to go
Up and away at will, and alone is free—

All else amidst the cannonading falls,
And as the harvest that their season bore,
The fallen lie along earth's open halls,
In the endless autumn of the Civil War.

## 9. ONE MAN

*The ocean*
*has no meaning*
*to anyone who has never*
*cupped in his hands*
*a lift of water.*

*The war has no meaning*
*until*
*a hundred thousand soldiers*
*are seen*
*as one.*

# 2.

# The Casualty

ARGUMENT:
*The Farmer and His Wife Have*
*Lost Their Son in the War.*

What hangs heavy
Among my bones?
My dead son there,
He hangs like stones.

He hung there living
A long time ago.
I dreamed his life.
I bade him grow.

§

My husband's eyes
Are like my boy's.
His humors shine
Like darling toys.

Many a mother
Fetches pain
By look of the father
With whom she's lain.

§

The life of a boy
Is like sweet loot,
My son in the orchard
Ripened like fruit,

By the orchard wall
He drank of the spring,
All love was charmed
By his everything.

§

I sleep at night
And in second birth
My soldier boy
Restores his earth.

He walks again
By the orchard wall,
His peach-gold face
Is summer's fall.

§

I wake in mourning
And I know the truth—
The war is a mother
That takes back youth.

## 11. THE FARMER

Rackily I walk across my furrows
And jar my skeleton upon my wasted land.
I used to look to where the orchard burrows
Below the hill and see my ripening lad there stand.


I spit now upon the acid soil and linger
Listening as if there was a thing to hear.
My poor old wife no longer lifts a finger
And we wonder why he walked here so many a year.


It ain't so long ago the leaves he tended
Made bonfires while he dreamed within his
blood
But now the leaves are over him like a mended
Comforter that somehow comes to lie on mud.


My trees will bare themselves to the gold
October
And my wife and I will be a-shrivel to winter.
They say poor Mr Lincoln is sad and sober,
And I guess if he could he'd save us all, chip and
splinter.

Why, I'll pray with her? If she looks so to get
me to?
Lord, but she hallelu's to break a man's heart.
The only thing is to find me a task to set me to,
It don't signify what, so long's I manage to start.

Well, it says hallelujah myself when I look up
high,
The autumn is here, there is gold streaks in
the blue.
How well I remember the burning leaves blow-
ing by
And the blue smoke long drifting the browning
valley through!

There'll come a day when cannon won't be
blowing,
And your house won't flood the yard with
plastered stones.
My fool boy marched off like he knew where
he was going.
I guess the fact that he thought he knew is what
aches so in my bones.

## 12. THE NEIGHBOR

That I should stay and look for him
    The meadow lark decrees
With upward hint of cherubim,
    Wings folded in the leaves.


The goose-bone in the farmer's hand
    Lies thin and dry; the bane
Of evil weather for his land
    Hides in the withheld rain.


My road lies in the withered copse,
    Where water lurks too deep:
Those ghostly bushes train their hopes
    Of bloom in dusty sleep.


So does the farmer's lamp at night
    Humbly contain his prayer:
For peaceful plenty in the sight
    Of grain against the air;


For song of lark above his house,
    For heat, and then the shower;
For nourishment, long-loving spouse,
    And harvest in his hour;

That son with his own son be blessed
    To set the future striding,
And let a grandsire go to rest
    With memory abiding.


Alas! the gloomy underbrush
    Has roots above the damp.
Alleluia! in this hush
    For thought of lark and lamp!

## 13. SPRING WATER

*The farmer and his wife*
*so long as they live*
*will seek*
*their lost son*
*in each other,*
*whose eyes were like water*
*in the spring*
*down by*
*the orchard wall.*

## 14. The Lost Son

One day beneath the apple tree
I lay and watched the creek.
It stang me like the honey bee,
The sun upon my cheek.

The leaves put underwater lights
All over me as I lay.
My face turned hot at all the sights
Within my mind that day.

There was a cannonading there
That mumbled under Hell,
'Twas either far upon the air,
Or here when apples fell.

I could not tell, I only heard
The tunes of glory horning.
It does not even take a word
On such an August morning

To break a boy into a man
And have him jumping over
The orchard wall which used to span
His boundary as a rover.

§

The drums were also glory-bent
And other boys than I.
The very air I drank was sent
To drunken me to die.


So sweet and sad the bugle cried
That facing each to other,
I loved those other boys that died,
I took the live to brother.


Yes, was not that what glory was?
To risk so with the living?
And is not that what loving does?
To make life worth the giving?


The blue haze in the battle woods,
The moss that's hard with blood,
The soldier's honest earthly goods
Cut naked like a bud,


A dog one Sunday afternoon
That would not lick my hand:
Oh if I were a man too soon,
These grew me up to stand.

But love and glory, live or dead,
In all my dreams were one—
I even dreamed the Lord God said
In me His will be done.

§

Beneath another tree one day
They had me standing guard,
When Mr Lincoln came that way
And looked at me real hard.

He did not say a word, nor I.
We both stood in the shadow.
I did not ask him, would I die?
But now I wish I had o'.

He knew it then, that I would die,
And orchard boys beside me,
And what I saw within his eye
He did not need confide me.

For I was then as old as he,
My tart and sticky juices
Like apples ripe beneath the tree
Must go for rotting's uses.

§

Some time later, where I fell,
I lay there like a baby,
For several days as in a spell,
Or in an orchard, maybe.

My hands lay up above my head,
My eyes were shut, and smiling,
My legs were bent, and I was dead.

*The air was still beguiling.*

## 15. The Enemy

We met upon a leafy hill
Where the cold rain ran
And one of us was there to kill
A fellow man.

I never did forget your look—
You shook your head and fell,
And left me of the life I took
More than I can tell.

I don't know why
We happened to make up
To each other,
But one day
He had a letter
And a gift
From his mother.
He turned all hot
And dusty plum,
Sort of red with pleasure,
And like many a man in camp
Still had
A boyish measure
Of what was good
And needed
And worth the hidden longing.
With little passions
Of recollection thronging
All in his
Thinking heart,
He looked my way,
And saw me watching him,
As if I would say
That I, too,
Was a drifted morsel
Of human timber,

And I too
Had resolutions once fierce
But now limber,
And white dust on my face
Where I'd kissed the dirt,
And a silver ringing
In my ears
To remembered rifles alert.
I too had letters
Cradled in my thumping breast,
That I would read
Over and over
Till they confessed
What I begged of them—
That I was beloved and prayed for,
And promised
Unquenchable sweetnesses
That I was made for,
If only
I could get safely home again
And live my life.
All that:
To the soldier among men,
A wish is a wife.
Such things he could read
In me,
As I, in his truculent look,
Could read his story
And man's
In his body's living book.

§

Upon that day
When the letter
And the package arrived,
We said not much,
But were friends,
And whichever one survived,
We knew that with one another
We dared celebrate thought,
And love better
Our concealed wishes
Than the boredoms
That we fought.
Sometimes I could almost see
The rich thoughts
In his head.
They're living still
In me
Even now that he is dead.

§

I was a little older
And it seemed right
That I'd go first.
But he was like
A tingling apple
Ripe to wet life's thirst.
He had it in himself,

He loved
All life,
And never knew it.
That is an act of creation,
However you want to view it.
And so when he went to die
In a blue day's battle,
When everyone I knew
Went stumbling up
A rocky hill
Like cattle,
Not all of him died,
But only a kind of
Autumn taking,
A season's fall,
Crisp golden leaf,
A dying promise of waking.
I was his friend,
I wrote a letter
To his mother and father,
And I wondered
If they'd see that this
Was more than sorrow's bother.
But whether they did or no,
It was his death
That told his friend
What to save in living life
And what was made
To spend.

Ordinarily it might seem
He had little enough
To share.
That isn't the point,
He gave it all,
His giving free as air.

§

After the battle
I looked for him and
Never found him but
Was told
That halfway up the hill
When the afternoon
Was settling cold,
A bullet set him down,
And then further down,
But he tried to walk,
For he was a very young man,
And it seemed
Not yet time for death
To balk
His stride in life,
And leaf by leaf
He tried to climb
The littered hill.
I climbed it afterwards

And that took
An effort of my will.
But somehow doing it
Set him in someone's thought
Forever free.

Amen. Let him be.

## 17. Coursing Rivers

*Endless come the seasons*
*across the soldier's hill*
*that is humbled with rain,*
*and matter that falls*
*upon the earth*
*like the leaves of autumn*
*inscrutably sifts with the air*
*and in sleeping hunger*
*is eaten back by the earth.*


*Blessed be the blood*
*that runs*
*upon our fields,*
*and dear the bones*
*that whiten*
*into ash.*


*Those who go,*
*after love,*
*so confidently to die,*
*pledge their selfless knowledge*
*of life inexhaustible,*
*life vast and pure,*
*as the ocean*
*is vast and pure,*

*having received the rivers*
*one by one,*
*the coursing rivers,*
*bearing each*
*its bedded career.*

Believe me, he said with his blood,
Forget me, he said with his word.
What I believe is the flood
That out of his river he stirred,

His river of wandering toward me,
Out of his boyhood ravines,
Bringing as if to reward me
The soil of his lived-among scenes.

I was a bank of the river,
It slaked me and drew away by,
And though that stream was the giver,
It took what I am till I die.

## 19. The Soldier's Child

Never shall I behold him
Who spent me into being,
But where earth may enfold him,
There should I be praying,

For love was my first cause
And he the instrument—
Most tyrannical of laws,
Most fugitive content.

Eternity is his,
Who gave me night and day.
Now for their verities
In filial thanks I pray.

# 3.

## The President

## 20. RESPECT

*He to whom*
*it is permitted*
*to respect all life*
*never sees it*
*in the abstract,*
*or in numbers,*
*but in the*
*illimitable value*
*of a single person—*
*one man,*
*one woman,*
*one child.*
*Feeling the single heart,*
*knowing the single hope,*
*entering the single mind,*
*he feels with all hearts,*
*knows all hopes,*
*wonders with all minds,*
*and must then give himself*
*through the vision of one*
*to all.*

## 21. Father Abraham and the Recruit

*Johnny, did you say goodbye?*
　　Oh, yes father.
I kissed them one and all goodbye,
I said now don't you go and cry,
For I'll be homing by-and-by,
　　Oh, yes father.


*Johnny, did you march away?*
　　Oh, yes father.
The drum and bugle they did play,
I marched through all the summer's day,
I slept by night in new-mown hay,
　　Oh, yes father.


*Johnny, did you fight the war?*
　　Oh, yes father.
For that is what a soldier's for,
To listen to the cannon's roar,
And fight till he can fight no more,
　　Oh, yes father.

*Johnny, did you see the worst?*
    Oh, yes father.
I saw what rendered Cain accursed,
I saw what men will do athirst,
I wished that I had perished first,
    Oh, yes father.


*Johnny, did you see the best?*
    Oh, yes father.
The love that never is confessed,
That hankers in a soldier's breast,
To die if it will save the rest,
    Oh, yes father.


*Johnny, did you learn to pray?*
    Oh, yes father.
The times I didn't know my way,
Or if I'd go or if I'd stay,
Or live or die, I learned to pray,
    Oh, yes father.


*Johnny, did you live a life?*
    Oh, yes father.
There's sweetness even in the strife,
When feeling cuts you like a knife,
And sleep comes later like a wife,
    Oh, yes father.

*Johnny, did you come on home?*
    Oh, yes father.
The government, they brought me home,
And laid me underneath the loam,
And here I lie, no more to roam,
    Oh, yes father.

## 22. WARTIME EVENING—
##    THE WHITE HOUSE

At the end of afternoon,
When the telegraph shut down
The evening came too soon
To allow him time alone.

Callers would squint to see
The war news in his face,
And then look sharp if he
Tried to hide the trace

Of sorrows yet untold
From battlefields away.
But still he seemed to hold,
Measured by the day,

In the weariness-to-death
Of his exhausted length,
The unpremeditated faith
Which was his—and all our—strength.

They rang the bell and hey!
We ran away
Down the school hill
Tumble and spill,
To the railroad tracks.
The weeds in the cracks
Of the board walk blew
And as we ran, I flew, I flew!

Middle of the morning.
Flags adorning
The railroad station
In glory-different celebration.

I put my face down on the rails
To see if the deep ground deeply quails
At the coming of the President's special train.
Yes, and yes, it jars so plain!

They pulled me back
Off the track.
I jumped and jumped
And through my veins the glory pumped.

Engine? Smoke?
The crowd awoke
When the whistle soughed
Like a long sad cloud.


My heart came up into my mouth.
Look out, Rebs, I'm coming south!


—A little boy, but even so.
And the train coming, furious and slow,
And the President riding in the last car,
And till today he was far, so far,
Away from my town in the summer fields,
Where boys have hearts and glory yields
As filling crops as anywhere.


Look! The flags stand free in the air!


When I am a man will I ever see
Such love as shone that day in me?


Because listen! the train is here at last,
With a golden blast
Of sunny steam,
And a lovely scream
From her iron brakes.

Even so, the crowd forsakes
The depot shed
To go instead
Back to the rear
To see him clear.
The engine grunts and sweats and leaks.
The conductor streaks
To the telegraph office in the station.
Well! the absolutely whole and entire Nation
Centers around our town this day,
For a minute or two, by the right of way.


I climbed up for a second
For I reckoned
To look in the door of the last coach.
But they picked me off like a struggling roach
And stood me down with the crowd.
But I was allowed
To stay in front and look.
It all, the whole thing, only took
But a minute.
But I was in it.


The door opened and there he came—
Oh no, just that old brown man with a scare-
    crow frame?
*That* ain't him—I was thinkin'
To see Mr *Lincoln!*

But the men all took on yelling,
And there was no telling
What he thought up there on the railroad deck.
He slowly tickled his neck
With his finger and smiled, ready to speak.
But the engine let go a leak
Of steam and screeching.
"There'll be no speeching,"
He tried to say, and shook his hand
And our town band
Cut loose with a blare.
He got my stare.
He looked down at me and frowned
Like a farmer on the ground
Making a joke and trying to be serious and
    scary
When all the time he's feeling peart and
    merry.
Somebody poked me and said the President
    was making up to me.
I turned all hot and got my head down, making
    up to be
Just so indifferent I couldn't be bothered.
But I durn near smothered,
And I felt ashamed.
Then the crowd exclaimed.

The train with a jerk was moving out.
It gave a shout
And fussing forth with hooting,

It spun its wheels, and gave us all a sooting.
Mr Lincoln tipped his hat and waved—
And then I got saved,
For I was nigh to bursting,
My heart was dry from thirsting
For the dream that a boy would have
Of power and glory and greatness to salve
The need to roam
Away from the little, old, sore wounds you get
   at home,
Just from living,
And eternal forgiving.


The train was leaving!
And he believing
That I didn't know who he was or didn't care!
I hit the air
And took out fast as I could run
Under the smoky jubilee sun
After the President's special train.
It looked for a space as if I'd gain
On the clacketty-clack
On the shining track.
But it picked up fast and hastened its clatter,
But it didn't matter.
He leaned into the light and grinned
And I ran like the wind,
And he clapped and stomped,
And I puffed and romped,

And the engine blew,
And I did too,
And as long as I tried
He continued to ride
Where he would be
A sight to see
To beckon me.


I began a long journey on that day.
He never knew it, but he showed the way.

## 24. Duncan and Mr Lincoln

"After life's fitful fever he sleeps well"—
The reader said the words and closed the book,
And slowly brought himself from out a spell,
And slowly smiled and tried to change his look.

But those who listened felt a threading chill
And thought to make a joke to change his fate,
But in his tired face they read his will
To think of what must happen, soon or late.

Of men there is an order for whom dreams
Are shadows reaching toward the way ahead,
And such was he, and such his vision seems,
As waking, he walked knowing toward the dead.

## 25. THE DREAMING SLAVE

I came from God
Whose child I am
And God abides in me
But if I'm held
In bondage fast
Then neither is God free.

When I go to sleep
My God comes down
Comes down by the darkest tree
The waters quail
And the smoke dies off
And He bangs the drum for me.

Nobody's old
Or nobody's young
When sleep makes memory
I know things then
That I can't recall
Till night time turns me free.

The fire sings
And the herons dance
And God plays with us all
And the jungle laughs
And infants preach
And glory makes me fall.

I fall and pray
And no one's there
In the burning grasses' ring
But two hot flames
And one is me
And one is God my king.


And I know God
And He knows me
And fire and drum and love.
Forever ago
My fathers made
The soul I'm dreaming of.


Let me sleep
My jungle grant
My fire keep me pure
For if I wake
To be a slave
I have no other cure.


A man owns me
And dirt to dirt
He sets me to my task
He guards my flesh
For he bought it dear
And gives me all I ask

He gives me all
Except my soul
He gives me meat and water
And these are dear
If first is fed
The spirit God's own daughter.

But she can pass
In just one way
And the only way she can
Is God's rule
That here on earth
She flow from man to man.

So day long
Hard I work
An animal and dumb
And night time
I lay me down
And I am God's own drum.

He plays a mumble
And I hear
The song that I desire
In time to come
In children's lives
The spirit free as fire.

For someone comes
Within a throng
And no man knows his goal
He has no gold
To let him spend
And so spends of his soul.

Oh Abraham
Oh morning branch
Oh blowing back of night
Oh golden cloud
Oh river free
Oh wielder of God's might

Oh let me wake
And take my soul
And give it back to me
Give me day
And lose me night
And tell God He is free!

## 26. Reviewing Negro Troops Going South through Washington, April 26, 1864

And while the others
On the sidewalk stared
At him for what he did,
He gravely bared
His heavy head
To the chesty Negro ranks
And gave to them
His color-blinding thanks.

President Lincoln would pause and stand quite
   still,
Holding on to his coat collar near his shoul-
   ders,
His vision wandering elseward, his thought a
   hill
On which his troubles jutted up like boulders.


Nobody knows what he saw in that rocky mus-
   ing,
From which he returned in his eyes when
   someone spoke.
But he was like a dreamer still refusing
To yield up the dream that followed him when
   he awoke.


A sacrifice is never all fulfilled—
Thus his duty to know and to sustain.
Did he wander in the name of all the killed
On that hill where their memory fell like rain?

*Did you ramble in the wood,*
  *Abe, my boy?*
I got lost within the wood,
But there I listened as I stood,
And I learned everything I could,
  Said Abe the boy.

*Did you come round the river's bend,*
  *Young Abraham?*
I saw round the river's bend,
I saw what we'd have to fend,
And how to steer until the end,
  Said Abraham.

*Did you gaze at books, and wonder,*
  *As a hired man?*
Any book seemed all of wonder,
Strong enough to set asunder
This from that, almost like thunder,
  Said the hired man.

*Did you measure our own land,*
  *Mr Surveyor?*
I legged my chain across the land,
I studied late on what I spanned,
And so discovered where I'd stand,
  Said the surveyor.

*Did you seek the word of law,*
*Mr Attorney?*
I saw nature in the law,
And fate weighed heavy by a straw,
And it was my own life I saw,
Said the attorney.


*Did you ponder on the War,*
*Commander-in-Chief?*
I never could escape the War,
I knew what we were fighting for,
It beat within my very core,
Said the commander-in-chief.


*Did you know what had to come,*
*Mr President?*
I often dreamed of what might come,
But not where it was coming from,
I knew the numbers, not the sum,
Said the President.

Ah, mother of our lost children,
    Poor troubled wife,
How much have we been burden
    To each other's life?


At times Ophelia cries through you,
    Witless in grief—
If I were a tree I'd shelter you,
    With bough and leaf.


Oh, for your sake, Mary, poor one,
    Adrift in meadows,
Would I might go alone
    The victim of shadows.

I saw him thirty or forty times at least,
Now at the front, and then in Washington,
And though the artists tried and never ceased,
They never got his likeness, ary one.

Oh, you could always tell whose face they meant,
Bearded, gaunt, and brown, with shadowed eyes,
But his smile was slow to come, and when it went,
You felt the weather of foreboding skies.

They drew his frame and hung his arms like
    weights,
And made him look all caved in at the middle,
But could not see his company of Fates,
And could not trace in line his somber riddle.

And there's another thing they could not limn—
The thing he gave us of himself direct,
That lives within us as it lived in him,
And made more of us than we could expect.

He stood up once upon a parapet
A perfect target for the sniper's sights.
We hauled him down but he is standing yet
Within our gaze upon our inward heights.

## 31. The Last Photograph, April 9, 1865

From within his countenance
The weariness of war
Had made its withering advance
Hour after hour

All throughout those four years
Which bowed him as he grew,
And turned the error of his fears
Into the lasting true.

It was like a runnelled hill,
His face, and in his eyes
Lingered all the dying, till
Life seemed a stale surprise.

And then war's end, at last in view,
Erased death from his face,
And those who saw him lived anew,
And shared his autumn peace,

And thought how Indian Summer dwelled
Hazy after frost,
And how the bounty of its yield
Was worthy of its cost.

# POSTLUDE: Glory

*After a century*
*the mystery of him abides.*
*It is the mystery*
*common to all,*
*in its power*
*like that*
*of a river*
*whose origin lies far behind,*
*whose end we cannot know,*
*but whose passage*
*is our term of life.*

*Few men have been*
*who lived their term*
*for all.*

*Of such was he,*
*who never thought*
*of glory.*

# Notes & Comments

PROEM: THE CATAFALQUE: at about ten years of age I used to go to the Museum of the Buffalo Historical Society on Park Lake, a few blocks from the house of my family, every Saturday, and often on afternoons after school. One of the exhibits which most strongly and frequently attracted me was, as I recall, in an upstairs gallery. It was the catafalque on which President Lincoln's coffin lay in state during a stopover of his funeral train in Buffalo on its way from Washington to Springfield. I think that the childhood impression created in me by that piece of funerary furniture gave me a sense of Abraham Lincoln's reality, and set going for me a lifelong interest in and response to his history and its period.

§4: TINTYPE OF A PRIVATE OF THE FIFTEENTH GEORGIA INFANTRY: after a tintype from the collection of Mrs Walter B. Hill, reproduced in *Embattled Confederates: An Illustrated History of Southerners at War,* by Bell Irvin Wiley and Hirst D. Milhollen. New York, Harper and Row, 1964.

§5: COMMANDER DEATH; §6, A CANDLE IN THE WARD: suggested by various passages in *Specimen Days in America,* and *The Wound Dresser,* by Walt Whitman, and *Hospital Sketches,* by Louisa May Alcott.

§7: LAST WORDS IN A SOLDIER'S DIARY: Under the title, "Death of a Hero," Walt Whitman, in *Specimen Days in America,* noted that "Steward C. Glover, company E, 5th Wisconsin—was wounded May 5 [1864] in one of those fierce tussels [*sic*] of the Wilderness—died May 21—aged about 20. He was a small and beardless young man—a splendid soldier—in fact almost an ideal American, of his age. He had served nearly three years, and would have been entitled to a discharge in a few days. . . . He kept a little diary, like so many of the soldiers. On the day of his death he wrote the following in it, 'To-day the doctor says I must die—all is over with me—ah, so young to die.' On another blank leaf he pencill'd to his brother,

'Dear Brother Thomas, I have been brave but wicked
—pray for me.' ''

§10: THE FARMER'S WIFE; §11: THE FARMER; §14: THE
LOST SON; §16: THE SOLDIER'S COMRADE: in all of
these the theme of the orchard and its fruit occurs.
I was interested to find a parallel to this general theme
in a passage by Whitman which I came upon long
after these poems were written: "Alas! how many of
these healthy, rollicking young men will lie cold in
death before the apples ripen in the orchard."—Let-
ter to his mother, from Washington, June 30, 1863.
Quoted in *Walt Whitman's Civil War,* compiled and
edited from published and unpublished sources by
Walter Lowenfels, with the assistance of Nan Bray-
mer. Alfred A. Knopf, 1960.

§12: THE NEIGHBOR: originally published in slightly
different form in *Hound and Horn,* vol. IV, no. 1,
October–December, 1930.

§21: FATHER ABRAHAM AND THE RECRUIT: written to
serve as a Civil War ballad in the context of my
novel, *A Distant Trumpet,* Farrar, Straus, 1960. The
poem soon found currency with folk singers, a num-
ber of whom provided their own musical settings for
it, and sang it in public performances. Several artists
announced that they intended to record their own set-
tings of the ballad, until they were dissuaded by my
agents, in the interest of a previously copyrighted
musical setting of my text by Donald Berke.

§22: WARTIME EVENING—THE WHITE HOUSE. As this
is a simple atmospheric piece with mood as its subject,
I have taken liberties with historical fact. The War
Department telegraph did not shut down actually,
and the President went at all hours—even at mid-
night—to read the latest battle dispatches. He tried
not to be available to callers after three in the after-
noon, and often went for an airing with his wife in
their carriage. But the pull at him by people was
constant, and as the War went on, he was increasingly

weary. Yet he was able to say, as quoted by Benjamin Thomas in *Abraham Lincoln, a Biography,* Alfred A. Knopf, 1952: "They do not want much, and they get very little . . . I know how I would feel in their place," and he received as many visitors daily as he possibly could. Thomas says, "His secretaries estimated that he spent at least three quarters of his time in meeting people . . ." The final point of the poem—the President's "unpremeditated faith"— echoes what many felt and some spoke of. Thomas refers to his "unwavering faith in the nation's destiny," and quotes a tribute written to Lincoln on July 6, 1862, by the landscape architect Frederick Law Olmstead: "In the general gloom, there are two points of consolation and hope which grow brighter and brighter . . . One is the trustworthy patriotic devotion of the solid, industrious, homekeeping people of the country; the other, the love and confidence constantly growing stronger, between these people and their president. Here is the key to a vast reserved strength, and in this rests our last hope for our country."

§23: THE SCHOOLBOY. Out of this lyric narrative grew the first important episode of my novel *A Distant Trumpet.*

§24: DUNCAN AND MR LINCOLN. During the last weeks of his life, President Lincoln reflected a sense of foreboding destiny to those around him, reporting dreams that concerned death, especially the famous one in which he saw himself lying in state in the East Room of the White House where a grieving throng was gathered. On Sunday, April 9, 1865, the last Sunday of his life, he was returning to Washington from City Point, Virginia, on board the presidential steamer *River Queen,* following a conference on the end of the War, which was at last in sight. Senator Charles Sumner was among those with him, and reported that the President held "a beautiful quarto copy of Shakes-

peare in his hands'' and read aloud the passage from
*Macbeth,* his favorite play, that consists of these lines:

   —Duncan is in his grave;
After life's fitful fever he sleeps well;
Treason has done its worst: nor steel, nor poison,
Malice domestic, foreign levy, nothing
Can touch him further.

(Edward L. Pierce, *Memoir and Letters of Charles
Sumner,* Boston, Roberts Brothers, 1893). On the
same occasion, the President repeated some stanzas
from Longfellow's "Resignation," which was said to
be a favorite poem of his. Its tone and matter sustain
the melancholy cast of Lincoln's thoughts at the time:
as the first stanza may indicate: "The air is full of
farewells to the dying,/And mournings for the dead;/
The heart of Rachel, for her children crying,/Will not
be comforted." Finally, according to an anecdote re-
corded by Charles Dickens and quoted in *Lincoln
Talks,* by Emmanuel Hertz, Viking Press, 1939, the
President said to his Cabinet members at his last meet-
ing with them on April 14, 1865, " 'Gentlemen,
something very extraordinary is going to happen
and that very soon.' To which the Attorney General
had observed, 'Something very good, I hope, sir?'
when the President answered very gravely, 'I don't
know—I don't know. But it will happen and shortly,
too.' " The President then spoke of a dream he had
had three times, of being " 'in a boat on a great,
broad, rolling river—and I am in a boat—and I drift
—and I drift—but this is not business . . . let us
proceed to business, gentlemen.' "

§26: REVIEWING NEGRO TROOPS GOING SOUTH THROUGH
WASHINGTON, APRIL 26, 1864: As he reported to his
mother in a letter quoted in Lowenfels (*op. cit.*), Walt
Whitman watched the Negro regiments who marched
with white troops in the 9th Corps. Lincoln was
present, and Whitman wrote, "It looked funny to

see the President standing with hat off to them just the same as [to?] the rest as they passed by."

§27: THE HILL: John G. Nicolay and John Hay, in their monumental life of Lincoln, recorded the impression of a caller at the White House who in referring to the President spoke of his "abstract and serious eyes, which seemed withdrawn to an inner sanctuary of thought, sitting in judgement on the scene and feeling its far reach into the future." (Quoted in Thomas, *op. cit.*) Hay himself said of Lincoln that "the eye grew veiled by constant meditation on momentous subjects; the air of reserve and detachment from his surroundings increased." (Quoted in *The Lincoln Reader*, edited by Paul M. Angle, Rand McNally, 1964).

§29: THOUGHT OF MARY LINCOLN: Mrs Lincoln's proneness to hysteria deeply touched and concerned her husband. After their son Willie died her grief was so intemperate and incessant that one day during one of her seizures the President led her to the window, and said, "Mother, do you see that large, white building on the hill yonder? Try to control your grief, or it will drive you mad, and we may have to send you there"— it was the asylum for the insane in the distance. (Elizabeth Keckley, *Behind the Scenes*, Carleton, 1868. Quoted in Angle, *op. cit.*)

§30: A VETERAN'S MEMORY: Suggested by observations of Whitman in *Specimen Days in America*, Oxford University Press, 1931. "I see the President almost every day," wrote Whitman, who saw Lincoln pass by on horseback or in a carriage on his way from the Old Soldiers' Home on the outskirts of Washington to the White House for his day's work. "None of the artists has caught the deep, though subtle and indirect expression of this man's face. There is something else there. One of the great portrait painters of two or three centuries ago is needed." (August 12, 1853.) Again, in 1865, after the President's death, Whitman wrote, "The current portraits are all failures—most of them caricatures." My last stanza was suggested by the anecdote, widely known, and included by Thomas (*op. cit.*) of President Lincoln's appearance at the fortifications of Washington on July 11, 1864, which were under sustained and severe attack by Confederate forces. Wearing his familiar tall hat the President climbed up and stood on top of the earthworks, exposed to enemy fire. Suddenly a soldier nearby cried out, "Get down, you damn fool, before you get shot!" It was Captain Oliver Wendell Holmes Jr., who presumably had not, in the heat of the moment, recognized the President.

§31: THE LAST PHOTOGRAPH—APRIL 9, 1865: Nicolay and Hay as quoted in Angle (*op. cit.*) recorded how Lincoln's temperament and appearance changed under the burdens of the war. "He aged with great rapidity," they wrote. The Brady photographs and other wartime evidence show plainly the ravages of concern upon the President's face. But when peace was assured, though the good news could not remove age and care from his face, he seemed to those about him to give forth peace and promise from within himself. One who saw him, James Harlan, was quoted by Ida M. Tarbell in her *Life of Lincoln*, Lincoln Historical Society, 1902, as saying: "His whole appearance, poise and bearing had marvellously changed. He was in fact, transfigured. That indescribable sadness which had previously seemed to be an adamantine element of his very being, had been suddenly changed for an equally indescribable expression of serene joy, as if conscious that the great purpose of his life had been achieved." A strong sense of this beauty of expression was caught by Alexander Gardner in the last photograph ever taken of Abraham Lincoln alive. A reproduction of this likeness appears on the publisher's jacket of the present book.